HOWLING DOWN THE MOON

poems by

Judie Rae

Finishing Line Press
Georgetown, Kentucky

HOWLING DOWN
THE MOON

ACKNOWLEDGMENTS

"Vigil" *Albatross*
"Petty Crime" *On the Bus*
"On Fall Mornings" *Poetry Now*
"The Corset" *Sanskrit*
"Recognition" *On the Bus*
"Kid Games" *Truth and Lies That Press for Life*
"U Haul" *Truth and Lies That Press for Life*
"Breakfast Love" *Inscape*
"Climbing Mount Hope" *Current*
"Making the Bed with the Cat" *Current*
"Putting Poppy Down" *Persimmon Tree*

Publisher: Leah Maines
Editor: Christen Kincaid
Cover Art and Design: Julie Valin
Author Photo: Will Connell

Printed in the USA on acid-free paper.
Order online: www.finishinglinepress.com
also available on amazon.com

Author inquiries and mail orders:
Finishing Line Press
P. O. Box 1626
Georgetown, Kentucky 40324
U. S. A.

Table of Contents

ON TIMELESS WIND

VIGIL

To be still,
to sit patient
as trees
to watch a bobcat
cross the path
not by chance,
but design.
To know
what the willow
knows:
The call of quail,
the haunts of deer.

These are the times,
when the turtle slips
from rock,
traps the eye,
when light shatters
on iridescent shell
and bends
the sacred.

ON TIMELESS WIND

On a late summer day
I follow the turkey vultures,
count them drifting on air currents:
First eight, ten, then a coven
of the broad-winged birds floating
on timeless wind.

Through thistle, thorn, thrust
of stone I hike
to a lonely glade, to ancient oak
where under the broad boughs
in the dried grass
I see her—the doe,
eyes blank now
and a yard away,
The fawn.

Tiny hooves align in perfect symmetry.

I have come too late
to read the evidence.
Did birth smells alert
a predator to this spot
while the doe in silent terror
endured?

I have questions I cannot answer
and hope a verdict
I will never know.

What is, is, I tell myself,
not a sad miscarriage of fate
but the way things are.

The vultures circle and flap,
circle and flap,
In cadence.
In time.

DROUGHT

In a dry time
lost to wind and sadness
birds scour
the parched earth
while crickets rasp
their insect
love.

AMONGST THE ALDER

the willow,
the tamarind ripe
with the sour smell
of sorrow,
a woman sits
on the rocks
and watches the riffles
carry leaves, carry
caution
past her.

Hope paddles
a fine course
between
possibility and passion

And love is
the narrow strait
of her undoing,
the fool's gold
beneath her feet.

LILACS BLOOM

in a difficult spring.
Blossoms tossed by a harsh wind,
bruised by frost so cold
it cracks the earth
in dumb surprise.

ON DEER CREEK

Between rains I wander
fields
to take back my life—
pieces lost to necessity,
bits eaten by obligation.
Sinew gone slack,
soul worn thin.

At creek's edge
I discover
iris
planted, how long ago?

Who was this gardener?

I feel I know her,
hands caked with earth
clearing moss, stone,
taming a small speck
of land
in a private time.

I wonder,
did she smile
at the thought
of my discovery of her
fine, small gift?
Or was her toil
vain,
no mind to future
visitors to this glen?

No matter.
Perhaps she too
sought solace
in a quiet glade,
renewal
in water, tree,
rock,
without thought

to future
pleasure—
mine, or
hers.

The iris opens,
juts one diaphanous flower
between crag
and creek,
and catches light.

THE LAST BUTTERFLY

Some tried to warn us.
Few listened, until…
until the last butterfly
crawled the distance
between leaf and flower,
wings congealed in a bloody
mass, deformed
by our own misguided design.

Few listened, until
the last bird
fell from the sky.
Song silent,
blackened wings, useless
now, unable
to fly.

Few listened, until
the last baby
nursed on poisoned milk,
uttered a feeble
cry
and left us.

Too late
we listened.
Too late
we wept.

PETTY CRIME

I steal flowers.
This compulsion to act
is not harmless.
I am responsible for denuding
entire neighborhoods. I've
had to switch jogging routes
until the land recovers.
Acres of lilacs have been lost
to my hand.

I can't help it.
I'm in relationship.
Crocus call to me.
Roses shout my name.

No flasher flashing
has ever felt so exposed
or so guilty as that moment
when I lean down
to liberate flower from stem.

No robber robbing
has ever felt so vindicated
or so vainglorious
as that moment when I bouquet
my bounty, and the ranunculus,
the anemones wave curly heads,
bow ever so slightly
to thank me for saving them
from frost, felines, and the unrelenting
possibility of death
by dog piss.

Fool she who amasses splendor
in greedy fists, hoarding what
cannot be owned—
a beauty thief.

But justification
for petty crime is easy
when the prize
is one tentative tulip smile.

FAMILY MATTERS

THE CORSET

my grandmother wore
could stand upright
unassisted,
the stays so rigid I could feel
them through the housedresses
she favored.
I'd touch not flesh
but substance as unswerving
as she.

Every morning
was the same—
even during the heat
of Canadian summers
she'd rise,
fasten with rheumatic fingers
the endless hooks.

I'd watch, a bean-pole child,
as she strapped her ample body
into the straitlaced
straitjacket, leaning over
to arrange her large breasts
so they conformed
to the outline of her confinement.

Next, she'd attach
stockings to the garters
that hung like sleeping
insects around the base
of her girdle.

In a shallow bowl
on her dresser lay

extra stays, bone people
I played with, marching their sturdy
bodies across the silken cover
of my grandmother's bed,
the quilt stained with brown
shoe polish I, as a toddler,
found and spilled
on the downy quilt.

My immaculate grandmother kept it,
she said, because when I wasn't there
the comforter reminded her
of me.
It's such a small stain, eh?

I can feel yet the severe
girth of her body
entrapped in a bundle of bone,
though love spilled out,
see her as she gardened
so outfitted, burrs
catching on her dark hose
and on the laces of her
no-nonsense shoes.

She needed no corset
to keep her upright.
My grandmother was
as unyielding as the undergarment
she wore, holding firm in her
God, her family and flowers,
her commitment to enfold her grandchild
against her upright bosom.

Though the stays poked
tender skin, I said nothing,
glad to be held by this woman
who corseted me, whose wide arms
ceded just enough to accommodate
one small form.

THE TEST OF TIME

My eighteen- year-old granddaughter
proudly lifts her shirt
to reveal a tattoo
that travels from her stomach
around her side
and up her back to her shoulder blades.

Despite my understanding of scarification
rituals, of rites of passage,
I am struck numb at the sight.

Age gives us some things
so what I say—when I finally
catch my breath—is,
Wow! That must have really hurt!

But what I want to say is,
When you're sixty....

*When you're sixty
that flower arrangement thing
around your navel is going to look like
Morning Glories after a hard frost.*

*And those fairies with wings aligned
a- lighting so airily
on a tendril or two?
Their wings are going to droop.*

*You think Tinker Bell
is ageless, don't you, kid?
Don't fool yourself; she's
really, really old,
probably even has age spots.*

Am I missing something here,
a new archetype
known only to the young?
A symbol, perhaps,
I'm just not getting?

Vines. Okay: youth, new beginnings.
Pain as transformative experience?
But isn't there enough pain in life
already?

Is it the art itself?
Some guy with needles and colored ink
transforming your body
into his masterpiece
only a very few—I hope—
will see?

What will you tell
your children?
How will they
up the ante—and they will—
on this?

I'm too old:
Bring back the days
of innocence: of rock n' roll
and poodle skirts,
a time when tattoos
were seen only on sailors
or ex cons.

A time when young women
necked a bit, partook
in serious groping in the back
seat of a '59 Ford, promised
love everlasting to the boy
who copped a feel.
But love and only love
was the excuse for presenting,
for revealing tender young skin
so fresh in its beauty
to another.

A time when grandmothers' lips
pinched at the sight of a too- tight

blouse on their granddaugthers'
chests, and didn't hesitate
to speak their piece,
to chastise a child
who violated unwritten codes
of womanhood.

It was all so clear then:
lines of demarcation
one dared not pass.

Art had its place in galleries,
in museums,
not on the backs of children.

STITCHING A LIFE
(For a grandchild unborn)

The Foundation Row: The first
stitch is patience; chain loosely.

Row 2: Slip stitch commitment.
Hook in humor and continue to end.

Next Row: Skip hatred,
and work around bitterness.
Repeat.

Back loop in books,
and dog and cat pals.
Measure in forgiveness;
yarn over prejudice,
edge with crimson sunrise.

Size with wonder
and dahlias large as dinner plates.
Mark with passion and thunderheads
and music.

Fringe in hopscotch and hikes
in the hills.
Join beach days with friends.

Seam with enthusiasm
and help for the poor.
Repeat.

Gauge with dreams realized,
and tears for tenderness.

Weave in idealism.
Block with laughter
and hammocks and swings.
Hand wash in kindness.

Finish with poetry,
wrapped in a blanket
of your mother's fierce love.

WHY I AM A VEGETARIAN

The stench
of the feed lot
outside Coalinga
hangs like fog
over Highway 5
and poisons
the air.

"What's that smell?"
my four-year-old grandson
asks my daughter
driving the distance
between Nevada City
and LA.
He holds his nose.

"*Cow poop,*" she says.
"*You know, cows?*
Hamburgers?"

There is silence
from the back seat
while my grandson
stares out the window
at the incarcerated beasts,
and processes this information.
Finally, thoughtfully,
he speaks.
"*Hamburgers are made*
from cow poop?"

CLIMBING MOUNT HOPE
For Hannah

It's a trek, isn't it, this journey into territory found on no map.
Uncharted land, often barren. Boulders everywhere.
Altitude sickness? Nothing to what you've faced.
The threat of avalanche. Imagine that ride: the whoosh of wind,
the call of birds amazed to see you fly, the white snow
perfect on a far-off hill.

You press on, latitude unknown. At this height
 weak sun bathes the landscape.

At the crest, clouds mask the horizon.
In the fading light, you come upon a flag
of many colors, a note attached. It reads:
Advice From a Fellow Traveler, One Who Loves You.
Dress warmly.
Take your meds.
Yell at the indifferent moon.
Enjoy the view, however fleeting.
Keep climbing.
Call home.

MAKING the BED with the CAT

"Oh, *this* game," he seems to say. "We've played
this before." He jumps on the sheets I've chosen,
scrunching his body under one, his teardrop
face peering out at me. "Ready?"
His lithe body primed, he makes a run for it, rushing
out of the room.

A minute later he is back, jumping on the bed
and scooting himself under the blanket, where
he hides for a time, a lump of feline.
"Get out of there," I tell him, moving
the covers. He ignores me and stretches,
his way of asking that I scratch his belly.
"Isn't this lovely?" he purrs. "Fresh sheets."

LOSSES AND GAINS

HEART BRUISED

The best day
was the one in the park
because sycamore is her
favorite word,
because the leaves
were as broad as babies' faces
and still she feels his back
against her back
and the damp ground of loving
through her jeans.

She can no longer make
grass sing like when
she was a kid and played
a tune for ladybugs.
She blames the grass.

It hurts to breathe.

OUTLASTING FROST

The spring that felt
like fall
with its relentless
rain and hail—
The spring
the tomatoes refused
to grow
and the corn seeds
rotted
in the earth.

That spring I thought
about my own roots
caught in a mire
of my own
making,
thought about
leaving you.

Instead, I moved
to a place
within
to guard what's left
of hope.
To wait, patient
in damp earth
like lilacs
whose time
will come.

U-HAUL

It's like moving furniture,
suddenly I get this urge to rearrange
things, and I won't rest
until it's done.

This is my life I'm talking about.
Like the living room,
the idea comes, I see my interior
in a new light
and all the dust balls have to go.

I could call a friend
but she has her own redecorating to do.
I could call him, but he never did
see the possibilities, even after I
explained in detail, itemized
the particulars until
the excitement was dead. Excitement,
damn it, exists in the imagined,
in the hope,
and only I
had too much of that.

So I grab the end of the heavy
leather couch, and I shove
and I push and I sweat
and I cry for all the times I hoped
alone,
for all the furniture I moved
alone,
because it was easier that way no questions asked
and I preferred it easier,
or maybe I was simply scared.

All this marriage has made me strong
and Bekins would grab me in a minute
to move pianos, to move
mountains, and even the house
isn't too big
for my pale,
thin,
Amazon arms.

FAULTY PARALLELISM

Love is not a grammar lesson.
The function of grammar is clarity, I tell my students
and see relief on their faces.
I was never one for diagramming;
the one sentence I mapped out to perfection
turned out to be a lie:

We will live in the future perfect.

Diagram this: There's been a mood shift
from the indicative
can you hear me?
to the imperative:
split the infinitive "to grieve".

A transition is needed
(to give examples)
in fact,
the restrictive clause—
the wife *who is always feeling hurt*
is essential to the meaning.

No more conjugating;
it's all past tense
anyhow
and nothing
can save us, *will save* us
from the stench of marriage done for,
leaping to fire, burning our skulls
with a thousand desert sorrows.

Future Conditional.

DENOUEMENT

I wanted something better than a lousy grade B movie
ending,
and you writing *FADE OUT*
in large letters, IN ALL CAPS
at the bottom
of the page.
Our page.

The only collaboration was the beginning
so why did I assume
you would be interested in finishing
this together,
rewriting the script, revising the story,
re-plotting the plot.

Why did I continue to hope we could get rid
of the bad guys
when
the only bad guys
were us?

UNCLAIMED PRESENT

I wanted to show you
where deer sleep.

HOWLING DOWN THE MOON

Sometimes love
is like howling
down the moon—
impossible, yet
we try, wish-filled,
hoping that
in time
we get it right.

BREAKFAST LOVE

The morning I burned the waffles
and he said *it's okay, I'd rather eat*
oatmeal
like Euell Gibbons, I really do
prefer the taste of cardboard,
honest, woman,
come here and together we'll down the cereal box,
together we'll devour crumbs, it doesn't make
any difference,
don't you know that?

That morning in a maple- syrup haze
I would have swallowed eggshells
and craved more
because the grin he gave me, the milk moustache
he wore
greased a path down my throat and nothing
was ever easier
to swallow,
it all went down like ice cream, like smooth liquor
and I would have eaten
the tablecloth
because with him
I realized
I could stomach it all.

RECOGNITION

For days I ponder
why
the space between
rolled shirt cuffs and watch
fill me with such longing,
why
I stared at sinewy muscle,
why
your watch worn crystal down
hurt.

My father wore his watch
that way.
I see him now, cuffs rolled
against the task,
thick arms sounding
sounding still.
Little girls ache for hands that bore us
skyward.
Women forsake too much for the return
journey.

Love is never pure—father love a burden.
Twist the wrist to the hour remembered,
approximate the past,
bring him back through shelter of other
arms.
Rewind memory.

Forgive me for knowing this:
Daddy hooked me.
Now,
impaled by you, tied
by dark, finely coiled
cords—your arms—
the spring of my slow turning.

KID GAMES

Moonstone Beach is a terrible place for a disagreement
and I never meant to have one, but the sun was just warm
enough and the wind in the lee of the rocks was hardly a wind
at all and the birds hung still above us, so what I said was,
We are moving through the speed of light.
That, he replied, *is impossible.* So to prove it I took him
by the hand and guided him to our room where we spun
back to the Pleistocene.
It was a terrific trip until afterward when he talked
of quarks and leptons and quantum mechanics so again I loved
him until his gluons came unglued and his toes curled like the toes
in Japanese erotic prints and I said,
Can too.
Cannot, he said. *It's impossible.*
Can too, can too. So then he called on Einstein and Stephen
Hawking and Heisenberg and I said *screw Heisenberg* and he
said, *I have other plans.*
Look, I told him. *Poets know certain things.*
I could see another theory headed my way so I kissed him again.
Give up yet?
Uncle, he gasped. *Uncle uncle* until he couldn't speak until his
elemental chemistry took a quantum leap, Simon Says take a giant
leap, mother may I? We are part of the immediate connection,
the implicate realm, electrons whirl, like sea birds we float in mid-air
see I told you so I am as old as crystal you can see right through
me moving through the speed of light.

WEDDING POEM
Answering Will

For nine winters we have loved,
now well, sometimes badly,
a love of smoke and fire.

In spring, the solace of lilacs,
in summer, the abundant rose.

I come to you now
as eager
as that first spring
when wild peonies bloomed
in the parched hills.

This love is remembrance:
of solace, of abundance,
of slaked thirst.

Hands that bleed into wood
bleed into heart not tamed
by time
or tempered by reason.

Our autumn nears, our fire
is seasoned
and love grows
beyond desire.

RESTING PLACE

Between the crest of your shoulder
blade
and neck,
a hollow
to cup my chin,
a place, a lovely ache.

There have been other aches:
a kitten asleep on my belly,
baby heads once snug
against collar bone
and breast.

But this spot, this small refuge,
this unknown gift you bring
in sleep
I could die in,
melt into mountain
beyond the window.
The peace,
the silent grace.

OFFERINGS

The curve of your leg
is like a smile you said.

Making love to you
is an unquenched thirst.
I could swallow the sea
and not be filled.

Yet,
at this moment
if the world stilled,
the look of your hands in fading light
would be enough.

THE STORM

wakes them,
the older ones,
light sleepers now.
They arise to close
car windows,
soothe the dog,
who trembles
with each clap of thunder.

Back in bed
they talk awhile,
fully awake, waiting
for the flash that precedes
the deafening boom.

In the white light
they reach out for bodies
well-memorized, slack now
with age, though still
grateful for tenderness
and touch.

The rain mounts
in intensity and matches
the pulsing hum
of their own
private rhythms.

SONGS OF SADNESS

COOKING FOR DEBORAH

She came to us as house sitter
and soon became far more.
The animals adored her,
recognized an old soul
in their midst.

The feral cat, fearful
of visitors, who preferred
the safety of night,
came when she called,
a mystery.
"I just spoke to her in French,"
she said, and the cat
wandered in.

We returned to bouquets
on the table, a joyous spread
as well: soups, bread, dessert.
In our absence the garden
flourished.

Cooking now for Deborah,
as she cooked for us,
who made meals out of delight,
gratitude, and shared them,
as we shared books and music
and laughter.

Poised now
between two worlds
we are thankful
for her special gifts:
this woman, this friend,
a grace note in our lives.

ITALIAN WINTER

In Anghiari,
in the green-lipped hills of Tuscany,
I witness the sadness of the old-age home.
Louisa takes me to the facility
where I see
the child-like drawings of Rosalina,
the eighty-year-old woman committed
fifty years ago by her husband after the birth
of their child.
"Post-partum depression," Louisa explains.
"They gave her shock treatments."
Rosalina draws butterflies and birds
in bright colors. Louisa tapes them
to thick plastered walls.

In another room a woman makes lace.
Swollen hands move wooden bobbins
in patterns known only to her,
a spider's web of thread, of mystery.
"She has no family," Louisa says.
"She has only her lace."

EDITH ON THE WING

My neighbor's mother joins us for dinner.
She listens to the conversation, smiles
occasionally, says little, gauging her words.
There is a cast in her eye, a turn of head
I recognize.

After dinner, she excuses herself.
"I'm tired," she says.
I ache to call after her, "Stay here and talk awhile."
I watch her long fingers, swollen, graceful, fold
her napkin. I watch her leave the room.

Her son watches too, calls after her, "Goodnight, Mother,"
then says, "When Edith was a young woman, she was a wing
walker. My father flew the plane while she walked."

The image haunts me:
Edith on the wing, gaunt, ethereal,
her precise steps from years before
transformed now to those we hear
shuffling down the hall,
slower, no less brave,
her life-long balancing
act,
perfected.

PUTTING POPPY DOWN

The rain has washed away your muddy
footprints from the driveway,
though cannot remove the indelible imprint
you made on our lives.

I have yet to clean the front door
glass where you sat, nose pressed to the window
and waited, anticipating our return,
your entire body dancing at our arrival.

No barks now, to warn that someone is approaching.
No low growl as you stand between us in the meadow,
warning us of bears in the field.

How you grieved your best friend, Edna cat,
panting all night, your loss as apparent
as ours.

In your absence, the other cats look around in confusion.
One has taken to sleeping
in the dark recesses of the closet.

There's a hole in the house.

The earth has shifted,
tilted on its axis,
swirling us closer
to the star you've become.

www.ingramcontent.com/pod-product-compliance
Lightning Source LLC
LaVergne TN
LVHW051608080426
835510LV00020B/3196

9 781646 621682